370.117 Bil 2016
Bilingual education
$25.00   ocn917888520

W9-DDM-507

HARRIS COUNTY PUBLIC LIBRARY

At Issue

Bilingual Education

WITHDRAWN

Other Books in the At Issue Series:

WITHDRAWN

At Issue

Bilingual Education

Noël Merino, Book Editor

GREENHAVEN PRESS
A part of Gale, Cengage Learning

GALE
CENGAGE Learning·

Farmington Hills, Mich • San Francisco • New York • Waterville, Maine
Meriden, Conn • Mason, Ohio • Chicago

Judy Galens, *Manager, Frontlist Acquisitions*

© 2016 Greenhaven Press, a part of Gale, Cengage Learning.

Gale and Greenhaven Press are registered trademarks used herein under license.

For more information, contact:
Greenhaven Press
27500 Drake Rd.
Farmington Hills, MI 48331-3535
Or you can visit our Internet site at gale.cengage.com

ALL RIGHTS RESERVED.
No part of this work covered by the copyright herein may be reproduced, transmitted, stored, or used in any form or by any means graphic, electronic, or mechanical, including but not limited to photocopying, recording, scanning, digitizing, taping, Web distribution, information networks, or information storage and retrieval systems, except as permitted under Section 107 or 108 of the 1976 United States Copyright Act, without the prior written permission of the publisher.

For product information and technology assistance, contact us at

Gale Customer Support, 1-800-877-4253
For permission to use material from this text or product, submit all requests online at www.cengage.com/permissions

Further permissions questions can be e-mailed to permissionrequest@cengage.com

Articles in Greenhaven Press anthologies are often edited for length to meet page requirements. In addition, original titles of these works are changed to clearly present the main thesis and to explicitly indicate the author's opinion. Every effort is made to ensure that Greenhaven Press accurately reflects the original intent of the authors. Every effort has been made to trace the owners of copyrighted material.

Cover image © Todd Davidson/Illustration Works/Corbis.

LIBRARY OF CONGRESS CATALOGING-IN-PUBLICATION DATA

Bilingual education / Noël Merino, Book Editor.
    pages cm. -- (At issue)
Includes bibliographical references and index.
ISBN 978-0-7377-7392-7 (hardcover) -- ISBN 978-0-7377-7393-4 (pbk.)
1. Education, Bilingual--Social aspects--United States. 2. Education, Bilingual--Study and teaching--United States. I. Merino, Noël, editor.
LC3731.B54545 2016
370.117'50973--dc23
                              2015027191

Printed in the United States of America
  1 2 3 4 5   20 19 18 17 16

Contents

Introduction

Bilingual education has not always been controversial in the United States. In the late nineteenth and early twentieth centuries, many parts of the country allowed bilingual education in public and private schools at the parents' request. At the turn of the century, approximately 4 percent of American children in elementary school had part or all of their instruction in German (the dominant second language at the time). During World War I (1914–1918), however, fears about loyalty caused the majority of states to enact English-only education laws. In fact, some states banned the study of foreign languages altogether. The study of foreign languages returned in 1923, after the US Supreme Court determined in *Meyer v. Nebraska* that such bans on learning foreign languages were unconstitutional under the Fourteenth Amendment, but it was a while before bilingual education resurfaced.

The Bilingual Education Act of 1968 came on the heels of the civil rights movement, intending to address the challenges that immigrant students were having in public schools as English language learners. The act provided school districts with federal funds for developing bilingual education programs. The programs developed and implemented over the next couple decades varied, some as one-way bilingual programs and others as two-way, or dual-language, bilingual programs. With one-way bilingual education, all students are English language learners who are taught in their native language (often Spanish) and English. Frequently in these programs the goal is to eventually eliminate the non-English language by teaching in a higher percentage of English each year until the other language is phased out. Two-way bilingual education, also called dual-language education, mixes native English speakers with native speakers of another language (often Spanish) and both groups become bilingual. In two-way programs, the goal is not to eliminate the use of the non-English language but to create fully bilingual students who have different native languages.

Currently, bilingual education is a contentious issue in the United States. Although requirements in school to learn a foreign language are rarely controversial, the education of schoolchildren in two languages is a polarizing issue. A great deal of the controversy arises from the fact that bilingual education in the United States developed out of a need to teach non-English-speaking immigrant children. Critics of bilingual education often believe that the practice is harmful to immigrants and that so-called English immersion, where non-English speaking students are immersed in the English language in order to learn it without instruction in their native tongue, is superior to bilingual education. Other critics of bilingual education contend that education in the United States should only be in English and that the country ought to formally declare English as the only official language.

According to a 2015 report by the Pew Research Center, of the fifty-four million Hispanics in the United States as of 2013, thirty-three million (68 percent) speak English proficiently: 89 percent of US-born Hispanics and only 34 percent of foreign-born Hispanics. However, almost thirty-six million (73 percent) say that they speak Spanish at home. Nonetheless, the Pew Research Center reports that English proficiency is increasing among foreign-born children. Furthermore, English proficiency rises as children and parents spend more time in the United States.

According to a poll conducted by Gallup in 2013, most Americans believe it is essential that immigrants living in the United States learn to speak English: 72 percent said it was essential, 24 percent believed it was important, 2 percent said it was not too important, and only 1 percent said it was not at all important. When asked how important it was for Americans to learn to speak a language other than English, only 20 percent said it was essential, 50 percent said it was important, 17 percent said it was not too important, and 11 percent said it was not at all important. When those polled were asked if they spoke a second language, 34 percent said that they did. Spanish was the most popular second language, followed by French and German.

The nation's ambivalence to bilingual education is reflected in California's Proposition 227. California had numerous bilingual education programs after the Bilingual Education Act of 1968 was passed, but that came to a halt in 1998 with the passage of Proposition 227. It mandated that students with limited English proficiency be taught almost entirely in English and eliminated funding for bilingual education. All English language learners must now be placed in at least one year of English immersion, but thereafter parents can opt for a two-way dual-language program if such a program is available (California has dual-language programs in Spanish, Mandarin, Korean, and other languages in various schools throughout the state). The popularity of dual-language bilingual education in California has caused the legislature to reconsider the issue. On the November 8, 2016, ballot will appear the California Multilingual Education Act, which would repeal most of Proposition 227.

As the viewpoints in *At Issue: Bilingual Education* illustrate, the debate about bilingual education is as contentious nationwide as it is in California.

1

Bilingual Education Should Be Increasing but It Is Declining

Stephen Palacios

Stephen Palacios is an executive vice president with the innovation consulting firm, Added Value Cheskin.

The benefits of being bilingual and the increase in US immigration support a growth of bilingualism in the country. But concerns about national identity and cost have led to a reduction in bilingual education rather than an increase. A middle ground in the debate may be possible as cultural norms shift with the rise in the number of bilingual and bicultural Hispanics residing in America.

Developments in social science, global trends and demographics all reinforce the significant benefits of bilingual education. Despite that, American schools show a steady decline in language programs. How can this be?

The Conditions for Bilingualism

First, let's look at the conditions for bilingualism. There have always been benefits to being able to speak more than one language; recent studies show the depth of those benefits: "Being bilingual, it turns out, makes you smarter. It can have a profound effect on your brain, improving cognitive skills not related to language and even shielding against dementia in old age."

Stephen Palacios, "Conditions Are Perfect For Bilingual Education—So Why Is It In Decline?" *Huffington Post* (blog), April 16, 2012. Copyright © 2012 Stephen Palacios. All rights reserved. Reproduced with permission.

The global economy benefits from a labor force that can transact business in more than one language, which would seem to reinforce the need for bilingual education. While English is the lingua franca [common language used among those who speak different languages] of today's global economy, it is hard to argue that knowing another language is a disadvantage in today's (or tomorrow's) market. Perhaps more than ever before in American history, knowledge of language and culture is a pillar of economic achievement.

The recent American immigration increase, mostly Hispanic, has created a large bilingual population. Certain school districts in major cities like Los Angeles or Houston would suggest that bilingual education is a natural evolution of our school systems.

While the United States does not have an "official" language, English is seen as a badge of American identity.

So, with all these conditions in place, bilingual education should be pervading our public schools. It isn't. In fact, it is going in reverse: "Thousands of public schools stopped teaching foreign languages in the last decade, according to a government-financed survey—dismal news for a nation that needs more linguists to conduct its global business and diplomacy."

The Two Factors That Explain the Decline

There are two major factors at work that help explain why—language as a badge of national identity and cost.

Language as national identity is a precept that extends to fundamental notions of nationalism. Often, language is seen as a badge of national identity—imagine a Frenchman who doesn't speak French. While the United States does not have an "official" language, English is seen as a badge of American identity. This notion has shown up many times over the course of our history, as seen with other waves of immigration that motivated the creation of Polish, German, Dutch, Czech and Norwegian language schools in the mid 1800s. This trend was fundamentally challenged during WWI [World War I, 1914–1918] (which related to the rise of nationalism), and a new psychology of English as a proxy for "American" arose. Unfortunately, language became a binary choice—English (which equaled American) or "other." This notion continues today, and is exacerbated by the latest rise in Hispanic immigration.

The second issue is cost. With great debates occurring in American public schools on the role of teacher unions, national education standards and the need to emphasize science and math, language has fallen by the wayside.

"In January 2002, Title VII of the Elementary and Secondary Education Act, also known as the Bilingual Education Act, was allowed to expire. It was eliminated as part of a larger 'school reform' effort of President [George W.] Bush's No Child Left Behind Act (Public Law 107–110) that abolishes most efforts at bilingual education and substitutes increased funding for English language acquisition efforts. The 34-year federal effort to investigate and experiment with bilingual education at the federal level has ended. Anti-bilingual education forces have won," according to StateUniversity.com.

A Possible Middle Ground

Is there a middle ground? Title VII originated with the intent of teaching non-native speakers in their language of origin, not as a notion of teaching all Americans another language. Can the United States adopt an approach that recognizes the English imperative (which is and always has been the language adopted by our citizenry to advance in society) and recognizes the increasingly obvious benefits of knowing another language? In the short term, the prospects don't look good, and bilingual education may be yet another societal victim to unresolved immigration issues. Implications to our economic competitiveness, our ability to experience the world more holistically, and even to age with less threat of Alzheimer's is at risk.

Reconciling American identity with a large ethnic influx has always been difficult. Perhaps as cultural norms shift, largely driven by the rise of bicultural and bilingual Hispanics, the issue of expanding the brain with two languages (or more!) can shift as well, to our benefit. *Espero que si* [I hope so].

2

Dual-Language Learning Programs Are Gaining in Popularity

Lesli A. Maxwell

Lesli A. Maxwell is an assistant managing editor for Education Week, *a magazine covering education news.*

Dual-language bilingual education—where students learn in two languages—are increasing in popularity. Texas and Utah have the most dual-language programs, concentrating on two-way Spanish-English immersion to serve the states' immigrant populations.

In a preschool class at Gardner Academy, a public elementary school near downtown San Jose [California], teacher Rosemary Zavala sketched a tree as she fired off questions about what plants need to grow. "*¿Qué necesitan las plantas?*" she asked her 4-year-old charges in Spanish.

"*Las flores toman agua*" was the exuberant answer from one girl, who said that flowers drink water. A boy answered in English: "I saw a tree in my yard."

The next day, Ms. Zavala's questions about plants would continue—but in English.

This classroom, with its steady stream of lively, vocabulary-laden conversations in Spanish and in English, is what many educators and advocates hope represents the future of lan-

Lesli A. Maxwell, "Momentum Builds for Dual-Language Learning," *Education Week*, vol. 31, no. 26, March 23, 2012, pp. 1, 16–17. Copyright © 2012 Education Week. All rights reserved. Reproduced with permission.

guage instruction in the United States for both English-language learners [ELLs] and native English-speakers.

The Growth of Dual-Language Bilingual Education

The numbers of dual-language-immersion programs like this one have been steadily growing in public schools over the past decade or so, rising to more than 2,000 in 2011–12, according to estimates from national experts.

That growth has come even as the numbers of transitional-bilingual-education programs shrank in the aftermath of heated, politically charged ballot initiatives pushing English immersion in states like Arizona, Massachusetts, and here in California.

Experts say the interest in dual-language programs now is driven by an increased demand for bilingual and biliterate workers and by educators who see positive impacts on academic achievement for both English-learners and students already fluent in English.

The goal is to establish strong literacy skills in English and Spanish in the early grades, and to produce fully bilingual, biliterate students by the end of elementary school.

In California—home to more than 1 million ELL students and some of the fiercest battles over bilingual education—the earlier controversies are showing signs of ebbing.

While the state's Proposition 227 ballot initiative, approved by voters in 1998, pushed districts to replace many bilingual education programs with English-immersion for English-learners, the state is now taking steps to encourage bilingualism for all students: Graduating seniors can earn a "seal of biliteracy" on their high school transcripts and diplomas, which signifies they have reached fluency in English and a second language. Last year, 6,000 graduates in the state earned the seal.

"The momentum behind these programs is really amazing," said Virginia P. Collier, a professor emeritus of education at George Mason University, in Virginia, who has studied dual-language programs extensively.

"And we are not talking about a remedial, separate program for English-learners or foreign-language programs just for students with picky parents," she said. "These are now mainstream programs where we're seeing a lot of integration of native speakers of the second language with students who are native English-speakers."

One-Way and Two-Way Immersion

Part of the 33,000-student San Jose Unified School District, Gardner Academy offers a two-way immersion program, in which native speakers of English and native speakers of Spanish learn both languages in the same classroom. Generally, to be considered a two-way program, at least one-third of the students must be native speakers of the second language.

Many of Ms. Zavala's 4-year-olds will continue to receive at least half their instruction in Spanish as they move into kindergarten, 1st grade, and beyond. The goal is to establish strong literacy skills in English and Spanish in the early grades, and to produce fully bilingual, biliterate students by the end of elementary school. Because of the state's Proposition 227 law, parents must "opt" for their children to enroll in the two-way program.

In one-way immersion, another form of dual-language learning, either native English-speakers or native speakers of the second language make up all or most of the students enrolled and instruction takes place in two languages.

The number of one-way and two-way programs is roughly equal, according to Leonides Gómez, an education professor at the University of Texas-Pan American in Edinburg, Texas, who developed a two-way-immersion model that is widely used in the state's public schools.

There are variations in how dual-language programs work, but all of them share a few hallmark features.

At least half the instructional time is spent in the second language, although in the early grades, it may take up as much as 90 percent. There must also be distinct separation of the two languages, unlike in transitional bilingual education, in which teachers and students alike mix their use of both languages.

Spanish is by far the most prevalent second language taught in dual programs, followed by Mandarin Chinese and French, according to national language experts.

For English-language learners, the dual-immersion experience is dramatically different from that in most other bilingual education programs, in which teachers use the native language to help teach English with the goal of moving students into regular classes as quickly as possible, said Mr. Gómez, who serves on the board of the National Association for Bilingual Education, or NABE.

"The goal isn't to run away from one language or another, but to really educate the child in both and to use the native language as a resource and an asset," said Mr. Gómez. "Content is content, and skills are skills. When you learn both in two or more languages, it moves you to a different level of comprehension, capacity, and brain elasticity."

The Role of Motivation

Research examining the effects of dual-language programs has shown some promising results for years, although there is not consensus that it's the best method for teaching English-language learners. One problem with discerning the effect of dual-language methods is determining how much self-selection is a factor. All such programs are programs of choice, with students and their families having the motivation to opt for the dual-language route.

Another factor is the great variability among dual-language programs.

Several studies in recent years have demonstrated that ELL students and other frequently low-performing groups . . . do well in dual-language programs.

"I think many of the new programs aren't able to achieve the ideal conditions for them to truly work, especially for English-learners," said Don Soifer, the executive vice president of the Lexington Institute, a think tank in Arlington, Va., that generally supports English immersion for the teaching of English-learners.

For starters, Mr. Soifer said, finding teachers is a major challenge because they need strong skills in two languages, as well as subject-matter competence. He said it's also necessary for two-way programs to have an even balance of native English-speakers, a feature that he says is difficult to achieve in some districts.

Still, several studies in recent years have demonstrated that ELL students and other frequently low-performing groups, such as African-American students, do well in dual-language programs.

Ms. Collier and her research partner, Wayne P. Thomas, found in a 2002 study that ELLs in dual-language programs were able to close the achievement gap with their native English-speaking peers, and that the programs achieved important intangible goals, such as increased parental involvement. The study examined 20 years of data on ELLs in 15 states who were enrolled in dual-language, transitional-bilingual-education, and English-only programs.

Ms. Collier and Mr. Thomas are also conducting an ongoing study of students in two-way dual-language programs, most of them in Spanish and English, in North Carolina. The researchers have found so far that gaps in reading and math achievement between English-learners enrolled in dual-language classes and their white peers who are native English-speakers are smaller than gaps between ELLs who are not in such classes and white students.

The data are also showing that English-speaking African-American students who are in dual-language programs are outscoring black peers who are in non-dual classrooms, Ms. Collier said.

States Leading the Nation

Texas has more dual-language immersion programs than any other state—with between 700 and 800 of them in schools—including some of the most mature, according to several experts.

Utah is a small state and, for our future economic development and the national security of our country, we have to educate students who are multilingual.

One district in the state's Rio Grande Valley along the Mexican border—the Pharr-San Juan-Alamo Independent School District—is likely to become the nation's first to have dual-language programs in all its schools, including middle and high school, Mr. Gómez said. In June [2012], the fourth cohort of students who have been in dual language since kindergarten will graduate from the district's four high schools.

In Utah, a statewide dual-language-immersion initiative funded through the legislature—the first such broad-scale effort in the United States, according to experts—is now in its third year, said Gregg Roberts, a specialist in world languages and dual-language immersion for the state office of education.

By next fall, public elementary schools across Utah will offer 80 programs under the state initiative, with roughly 15,000 students enrolled in Spanish, Mandarin, French, and Portuguese. The goal is to have 30,000 students enrolled in 100 programs by 2014, Mr. Roberts said.

"Utah is a small state and, for our future economic development and the national security of our country, we have to educate students who are multilingual," he said. "There is broad agreement in our state about that. It's not a red or a blue issue here."

Many of Utah's programs so far are two-way Spanish-English immersion, drawing on the state's growing Latino immigrant community, said Myriam Met, an expert on immersion programs who is working closely with Utah officials on the initiative.

But the most in-demand programs in Utah are Mandarin. Ms. Met said there were fewer than 10 Chinese immersion programs in the nation in 2000. The current estimate stands at 75 Chinese programs, and by next fall, roughly a quarter of those will be in Utah, she said.

Some of the nation's oldest Chinese programs are offered in the 56,000-student San Francisco [California] public schools.

Most students start in one of the city's five elementary schools, where they split instructional time between English and Cantonese or English and Mandarin. Eventually, many end up at Abraham Lincoln High School, where a mix of native Chinese-speakers and students who have been in the immersion program since the early grades take advanced Chinese-language courses, in addition to at least two content-area courses each year in Cantonese.

Amber Sevilla, a 14-year-old freshman in the Chinese-immersion program at Lincoln, is fluent in English, Cantonese, and Mandarin. She has been in Chinese immersion since kindergarten and learned some Chinese at home from her grandmother. Through middle school, nearly all her instruction was conducted in Chinese, including math. Currently, she is taking health education and college and career education in Chinese.

"I'm excited that I can count on being bilingual and biliterate as I go to college, and I know it's going to be an advantage for me even though I don't know yet what I want to do for my career," said Ms. Sevilla. "It's hard work, but it's worth it."

Like nearly all her classmates in the immersion program, Ms. Sevilla is on track to earn California's new state seal of biliteracy.

The Benefits of Dual-Language Programs

Rosa Molina, the executive director of Two-Way CABE, an advocacy group for dual-language programs that is an affiliate of the California Association for Bilingual Education [CABE], said students like Ms. Sevilla benefit in multiple ways.

"They preserve their primary language or their heritage language, they develop a broader worldview that they take into college and the work world, and they gain huge advantages in their cognitive development that translates into flexibility in their thinking and the ability to successfully tackle really rigorous coursework," Ms. Molina said.

Advocates for English-learners emphasize the importance of expanding programs that are truly two-way and fully accessible to ELLs. Laurie Olsen, a national expert on English-learners who designed the instructional model in use at the Gardner Academy in San Jose, cautions against allowing programs to become dominated by middle- and upper-income students whose parents want them to learn a second language. If that happens, she said, one of the most promising approaches to closing the achievement gap between English-learners and fluent English-speakers will be squandered.

"We know that English-learners who develop proficiency in their home language do better in English and in accessing academic content," she said. "Yet we still live in a world where the belief is wide that English should be enough."

Bilingualism Can Help Close Learning Gaps for Immigrant Students

Elahe Izadi

Elahe Izadi is a general assignment national reporter for The Washington Post.

Research shows that the brain gets cognitive benefits from being bilingual regardless of socioeconomic status. Thus, encouraging bilingualism can help close the gap between poorer immigrant children and native English speakers.

The gospel of the day is that raising children to speak and understand more than one language is good for their cognitive development. A number of studies released in the past few years have indicated that multilingual speakers may even have more focused brains and higher processing abilities. Not surprisingly, this research—and the media attention that has accompanied it—has led to renewed efforts among more-affluent parents to secure spots for their children in language immersion schools and employ multilingual nannies who can expose their wee ones to another language from the earliest ages.

The Benefits of Bilingualism

A skeptic might ask, however, if it's possible that the cognitive benefits such bilingual children receive are more a result of

Elahe Izadi, "Bilingualism Can Help Close Learning Gaps for Immigrant Students," *National Journal*, April 30, 2014. Copyright © 2014 National Journal. All rights reserved. Reproduced with permission.

their privileged socioeconomic status—and the resources they have access to—rather than simply an ability to converse in Spanish or Mandarin.

The encouraging answer is: not really.

Studies show that the brain does indeed gain cognitive benefits from being bilingual, regardless of one's socioeconomic status. And that has potentially significant implications in the United States, where native bilinguals tend to be poorer than the general population.

It helps to understand what, exactly, you gain from speaking more than one language. The benefit is quite specific to a very important aspect of our brain's functioning, says Ellen Bialystok, a cognitive neuroscientist at York University in Toronto [Canada] who has been examining bilingualism's effects on the mind for decades.

Being bilingual improves the executive functioning processes that manage things such as attention, working memory, planning, and problem-solving. The bilingual mind experiences a workout from constantly suppressing one language while activating another, which builds up the brain's cognitive processes.

Overall, kids from poorer socioeconomic backgrounds tend to perform worse than wealthier kids on executive functioning measures. Bilingualism, it appears, can help compensate for that gap.

"This is the most important cognitive system we have," Bialystok says. "There are studies showing that executive function in childhood predicts academic outcomes in a narrow sense, and broader success outcomes in life."

What the Research Shows

But when Bialystok started doing research on the bilingual effect, there was a concern that socioeconomic factors were interfering with the results. Now there are a number of studies that, when taken together, she says "rule out that our effects are limited to a certain socioeconomic status, or even worse, confounded by socioeconomic status and not reflecting the effects of bilingualism."

One study Bialystok was involved with looked at a group of low-income children from a specific region of Portugal. On a litany of tests, measuring things like intelligence and visual memory, the kids who stayed in Portugal and those who had immigrated to Luxembourg and learned to speak Luxembourg-ish performed the same. But on the measures that test the brain's control function, researchers found that the kids in Luxembourg "significantly outperformed those who stayed behind," Bialystok says.

Overall, kids from poorer socioeconomic backgrounds tend to perform worse than wealthier kids on executive functioning measures. Bilingualism, it appears, can help compensate for that gap.

A separate 2008 study from University of Washington researchers compared Spanish-English native bilingual kindergarteners (who tended to come from more disadvantaged backgrounds) to English speakers enrolled in second-language immersion and English-only speakers. The native bilinguals outperformed the other groups on executive function tests. But that was only after controlling for factors like socioeconomic status; before doing that, their scores were the same. Given the impact of socioeconomic and other factors on cognitive development, those kids should have done worse than their more-advantaged peers. Essentially, disadvantaged bilinguals may be "doing more with less," the researchers noted.

That study was particularly notable because after English, Spanish is by far the most common spoken language in the U.S. About 60 million people, or one in five, speak a language other than English at home, according to 2011 Census data.

And 21 percent of them live below the poverty line, compared to just 14 percent of the general population.

Myths still persist around bilingualism. For a long time, educational experts concluded that it took bilingual kids much longer to develop language skills, says Sarah Roseberry Lytle, the director of translation at the University of Washington's Institute for Learning and Brain Sciences. It turns out that's not the case; it just looked that way when those kids were assessed in only one language.

Closing the Gap

Support for bilingual or multilingual education continues to grow, even where it was once viewed with suspicion. California, for instance, is now home to an explosion of dual-language immersion programs, where 5-year-olds learn in Italian and Japanese. But as recently as 1998, California voters banned bilingual-education programs, mandating that students whose first language was not English be taught "overwhelmingly in English." Since then, the gap in test scores between those students and native English speakers has widened.

Encouraging bilingualism could help toward closing that gap. While "there is no benefit of bilingualism with general IQ and things like that," says Lytle, "if you think about the structure of a classroom day, kids are often asked to switch tasks pretty quickly without retention time. The idea is that bilingual kids are going to be better at task-switching."

But being bilingual doesn't exist in a vacuum for many children, particularly those who come from poorer socioeconomic situations. And having to deal with societal factors that discourage or don't value bilingualism can harm them, says Afra Hersi, a literacy education professor at Loyola University Maryland who has researched bilingual teenagers and their school experiences. "Bilingualism as a distinct advantage is not valued as much in the United States if you are a child from a low socioeconomic circumstance," she says.

There are complicating factors within immigrant communities, as well. Immigrant kids tend to pick up English quicker than their parents, "which puts strains on the family cohesion," says Hersi. "It puts parents and children at odds with each other."

Overall, though, there is a benefit to being bilingual from which everyone, regardless of socioeconomic status, stands to gain—particularly if speaking two languages is seen as a good thing. The bilingual benefit doesn't guarantee greater academic achievement, admission to college, or a high-paying job—but it certainly sets the foundation for greater successes in life.

4

Bilingual Education Has Failed to Help Non-English Speakers

ProEnglish

ProEnglish is an organization that advocates English as the official language of the United States and of individual states and opposes the practice of bilingual education in schools.

After thirty years of bilingual education programs in the United States, the research shows that these programs fail to teach English to English-language learners. English immersion programs, where students are taught in English, work best.

Bilingual education is the practice of teaching non-English-speaking children in their native language, while they are learning English. Developed in the 1970's, the basic idea was to teach the school subjects—math, science, social studies—in the child's first language so the child would not fall behind his English-speaking classmates. English language lessons were also provided. Bilingual children were schooled apart from English speakers for most of the school day for several years, a substantially separate and costly education.

The Research About Bilingual Education

After 30 years of the bilingual experiment and billions of dollars spent, reliable research shows that these programs fail to teach students the English language and literacy they need for school success. The idea was well-intentioned, but it has

ProEnglish, "Bilingual Education," ProEnglish. Copyright © 2010 ProEnglish. All rights reserved. Reproduced with permission.

proven to be a failure. Segregation by language and ethnicity does not lead to higher academic performance, does not raise students' self-esteem, results in social isolation and may contribute to high drop-out rates. Delaying the learning of English, the language of school and community life, holds back student achievement. Graduating from high school without fluency and literacy in English deprives students of opportunity in an English-speaking country.

ProEnglish supported state initiatives to end bilingual education. Voters in three states that had long years of experience with bilingual programs gave strong approval to the "English for the Children" initiative to replace bilingual education with English Immersion teaching. California in 1998 gave 60% voter approval to the change; Arizona voters gave 62% approval in 2000; and in Massachusetts in 2002 a 68% majority voted for change. At present only three states still require bilingual education: Texas, Illinois and New Jersey. Teaching American children another language is laudable, but is an entirely different issue. ProEnglish believes it is the responsibility of our public schools to teach non-English-speaking children English as rapidly as possible.

Thirty years of research shows that bilingual education [does] not lead to faster or better learning of English.

English Immersion programs, now called "Structured English Immersion (SEI)" work best. In these programs, students spend one full school year (or longer, if necessary) studying the English language—learning to speak, read, and write, and to master the vocabulary they need to learn school subjects taught in English. As soon as students are skilled in English, they join their classmates in regular classrooms where all teaching is in English. Both in California and Arizona, state test reports show students learning English in an average of two years, and achieving passing scores on reading and math tests as well. These results are not unusual.

In a Lexington Institute study published in 2008, it is reported that some of the highest-performing students in California public schools are children who started kindergarten with little or no English. In June 2009, Massachusetts proudly announced that in seventeen of the forty-two Boston high schools the valedictorian of the graduating class was a student who had come from another country within the past few years, without any knowledge of English. With English Immersion support, these students not only learned English rapidly but were able to achieve success in high school classes at a high level.

In California, Superintendent of Schools Ken Noonan, former head of the California Association for Bilingual Education, changed his mind completely after the first year of English Immersion in his schools. When he saw how quickly the students learned English and school subjects taught in English, he became a vocal supporter of English language programs.

The Justification for Bilingual Education

Thirty years of research shows that bilingual education:

- Does not lead to faster or better learning of English

- Does not lead to better learning of school subjects, and

- Does not produce higher self-esteem in students.

The first two items were, indeed, the original expectations of the laws passed. A politically powerful bureaucracy continues to promote these programs for ideological reasons, for higher school funding and extra teaching jobs. Some educators promote bilingual education as a way of "maintaining one's native language and culture." That is not the responsibility of our public schools but of the family and community.

With 327 languages represented in the U.S. today, the mission of our schools is not to maintain family languages but to give students the tools to succeed as productive citizens.

Politicians fear any vote against bilingual education will mark them as hostile to minorities. But millions of people in three states voted for English language teaching, including substantial numbers from immigrant communities, a sign that politicians are out of step with the people they represent. A READ Institute survey showed 81% of Hispanics want their children to learn English quickly; only 12% wanted their children taught in Spanish, one of many surveys showing such attitudes. Immigrants come to this country seeking to thrive in our society, yet our public schools often fail to give them the skills needed to prosper and participate in our democratic discourse.

The Current Status of Education for Non-English Speaking Students

States with substantial numbers of English Language Learners report the following data on school enrollment and educational practices:

[California was the] first to overturn bilingual programs by voter initiative. . . . [Since then] the state has documented steadily higher achievement for formerly ELL students on state tests of reading and math.

Arizona: Enrolls 7% of all English Learners in U.S. schools. Since changing to Structured English Immersion teaching in 2002, the state reports a consistent improvement in the school performance of ELL [English language learner] students. On average, students exit the English-teaching program in two years and have high passing rates on state tests of reading, math and writing. Arizona is leading other states in developing innovative curriculum for English teaching and for student success.

Alaska: State law requires bilingual/bicultural education for its population of Aleut and American Indian students.

California: First to overturn bilingual programs by voter initiative (1998) and home to the largest Spanish-speaking population of all states (51.4% reported in November 2010), the state has documented steadily higher achievement for formerly ELL students on state tests of reading and math. Three-fourths of the state's ELL students are in English Immersion programs.

Colorado: Only state to vote down an initiative to end bilingual programs in 2002. The state maintains Spanish bilingual programs.

Connecticut: Ended bilingual programs in 2000 for the mainly Spanish-speaking ELL students concentrated in the public schools of the three largest cities.

Florida: State law allows either bilingual or English as a Second Language (ESL) programs for its 300,000 English Learners.

Illinois: Retains its mandate for bilingual education. Enrolls about 200,000 ELL students.

Massachusetts: First in the U.S. to pass a law requiring bilingual teaching (Transitional Bilingual Education, 1971). The state referendum in 2002 brought in a complete change of education with 85% of ELLs now enrolled in English Immersion programs. Approximately 50,000 students are classified ELL. Scattered evidence of improved achievement for ELLs may be obtained from the Department of Education but no comprehensive study has yet been produced by the state.

Michigan: Like Florida, allows either bilingual or ESL programs but only provides state funding for bilingual education. That essentially removes any incentive for program choice.

Nevada: No law requires bilingual education for the high proportion of school children who are not fluent in English (1 in 4) and little is known of what is common practice.

New Jersey: Retains its bilingual education law for its mainly Spanish-speaking ELL students. There is no referendum process in this state.

New Mexico: Requires bilingual or ESL programs for its English Learners who constitute one in every four students in the public schools.

New York: Does not have a bilingual education law, allows either bilingual or ESL programs, and enrolls approximately 250,000 ELL students. A study conducted in the New York City Public Schools in the mid-1990s established the superior results of the English-teaching approach: students in ESL classes learned English and learned subject matter in English in 2–3 years; students in bilingual classes needed 6–7 years to reach the same levels of achievement and had a higher high school drop-out rate.

Texas: Mandates bilingual education for at least three years, and enrolls about 750,000 ELL students. Dr. Christine Rossell's 2009 study, "Does Bilingual Education Work? The Case of Texas" answers that question with a resounding, "No, it emphatically does not work better than ESL."

Court challenges to the English Immersion law in California did not succeed in overturning "English for the Children." Bilingual education is over in California, the state with half of the five million English Language Learners (ELL) in the country. The State of Arizona Department of Education has fought off attacks on its English Immersion programs in a case that was ruled favorably for the state in the U.S. Supreme Court in June 2009, *Flores vs. State of Arizona*. Across the country, bilingual education is no longer the default mode of teaching. The battle has largely been won, giving children the best avenue to an equal educational opportunity, reducing the segregation of English Learners and lowering spending for public education.

5

Bilingual Education in California Has Been Successful

Jill Tucker

Jill Tucker is an education reporter for the San Francisco Chronicle.

California created a ban on bilingual education without parental permission in 1998. Yet, for those parents who have chosen bilingual education for their children, the results have shown that bilingual education deserves the growing support it is receiving.

In the 15 years since voters essentially banned bilingual education in state schools, teaching English learners to read, write and do arithmetic first in their native language has nearly disappeared from California classrooms.

After the Ban on Bilingual Education

Since Proposition 227 overwhelmingly passed in June 1998, it's been all about learning English, first and foremost—but not in San Francisco. Nearly 30 percent of the city's 17,000 English learners are in bilingual education programs, compared with 5 percent on average statewide, according to the most recent data available.

And it's working, according to a recently published Stanford University study commissioned by the San Francisco Unified School District.

Republished with permission of *San Francisco Chronicle*, from "S.F. Seen as Model in Bilingual Education over English Only," by Jill Tucker, Copyright © 2014; permission conveyed through Copyright Clearance Center, Inc.

Districts can get around the Prop. 227 ban by having parents sign a waiver authorizing their children to be in bilingual education programs.

Bilingual education students, who learn to read and write in their native language and then transfer those academic skills into English, are—after a slower start—as fluent by sixth grade as those focused on and immersed in English with minimal support in their home language, according to the study.

The same results were seen with English learners in dual-immersion programs, which teach native English speakers and non-English speakers first in Spanish, Chinese, Arabic or other languages before phasing English into their studies.

In other words, students ended up equally proficient in English no matter how they learned it in San Francisco schools, the Stanford researchers found.

The difference is that those in dual-immersion and bilingual education programs are taught in those five or six years to speak, read and write in two languages and are more likely to be bilingual.

Despite the state ban, "we haven't actually deterred from our goal of bilingualism," said Christina Wong, San Francisco Unified's special assistant to the superintendent. "We were very pleased, and it really helps justify the investment the district has made over a number of years to this effort."

Policymakers are rethinking an English first approach and parents are calling for access to language-immersion programs.

The Reasoning for the Ban

When Prop. 227 passed, "bilingual" was, to many, a bad word.

There was a sense that in bilingual education classrooms, English learners were segregated and languished in native language classrooms, putting them at a significant disadvantage to their English-fluent peers.

Knowing English, supporters said, was critical—even if that meant purging a first language from a student's skill set.

"Bilingual education in California means monolingual instruction, mainly in Spanish," said the measure's author, Ron Unz, during the 1997–98 campaign. "It would be a very good thing if (students) were fluent in two languages, but often they come out illiterate in two languages. I've always been somebody very skeptical of bilingual education."

The initiative passed with 60 percent voter support.

More than 15 years later, the global economy increasingly has placed value on bilingual workers, whether English is their first or second language. That demand in the United States has trickled down into schools, where policymakers are rethinking an English first approach and parents are calling for access to language-immersion programs.

In 2012, several districts in California, including San Francisco, started offering a Seal of Biliteracy for graduating high school seniors to acknowledge their language skills.

Nationally, Secretary of Education Arne Duncan said last year [2013] that when teaching English to English learners, the primary language should be maintained so they can become bilingual.

"We are really squandering our linguistic resources by not supporting the primary-language instruction," said Sarah Capitelli, a University of San Francisco professor of teacher education. "I feel like it's a huge waste."

Esther Woo started teaching 10 years ago when Prop. 227 and the decline of bilingual education in California was in full swing.

The Demand for Bilingual Education

Prop. 227 "was all about assimilation into the dominant culture," said Woo, a fifth-grade Spanish dual-immersion teacher at San Francisco's Buena Vista Horace Mann K-8 school. "I feel now the focus is more student centered rather than policy centered.

"We're creating these successful citizens of the future."

While bilingual education has continued to thrive in San Francisco, parents of English learners are increasingly opting for the dual-immersion programs, which use the child's native language but don't require segregated classrooms.

Currently, San Francisco Unified has more than 5,000 students in dual-immersion programs who started as kindergarteners. Six years later, these middle schoolers are fluent in English and Cantonese, Spanish, Mandarin or Korean.

There is always more demand than seats in the classrooms.

Often, the English-speaking students have a family background in the language being taught, but through one or two generations, it was lost, Woo said. Their parents "wished they would have had that advantage."

While the Stanford study offered a generally positive review of district English-learner programs, with the vast majority of students reaching fluency by the end of middle school, the picture isn't entirely rosy in San Francisco.

The study showed that Chinese English learners reach fluency in greater numbers and faster compared with Spanish speakers, a trend that mirrors an achievement gap in test scores and other academic indicators between white and Asian students and Latino and African American students.

San Francisco might make a good case for bringing back bilingual education in California.

In addition, the graduation rate for English learners in San Francisco is 68 percent, compared with 82 percent districtwide, according to the California Department of Education.

Yet statewide, the graduation rate for English learners is 62 percent.

The Stanford study included about 18,000 English learners in San Francisco schools from 2002 to 2010 and examined their results on the California English Language Development

Test as well as the percentage of students who transitioned from English-learner status to full fluency each year.

A Change in Attitudes

All told, San Francisco might make a good case for bringing back bilingual education in California, given the results of the study. And research has consistently backed its effectiveness.

"The research is 100 percent solid in bilingual education," said Stephen Krashen, University of Southern California professor emeritus in linguistics. "Students in well-designed bilingual programs outperform comparison students on tests of English reading. Despite the overwhelming evidence, bilingual education is still not well supported."

He blames the bilingual education wars that swayed public opinion in California, Colorado and Massachusetts.

Still, there's a shift.

"I think the attitudes have changed," said Shelly Spiegel-Coleman, executive director of Californians Together, a coalition of parents and education civil rights groups.

Yet, so far, there has been little to no political effort to officially rescind Prop. 227 given that districts can get around it with a parent signature.

But would Prop. 227 still pass today?

Spiegel-Coleman said it still might despite the demand for bilingualism.

"I think the vote would be different," Spiegel-Coleman said. "I think it would be closer."

6

California's Ban on Bilingual Education Helped Immigrant Children

Ron Unz

Ron Unz drafted California's Proposition 227 and led the campaign for the 1998 passage of the initiative, which eliminated most of California's bilingual education programs.

Despite politician opposition to a ban on bilingual education, California voters approved Proposition 227 in 1998, which requires schools to teach English immediately to immigrant children. Despite the success of the educational policy, opponents are seeking to repeal Proposition 227 and reinstall bilingual education programs in the state's schools.

After almost seventeen years history may be about to repeat itself in California politics, though perhaps with a strong element of farce. Late last week [April 30, 2014], the Senate Education Committee voted 8-to-0 to place a measure on the November 2016 ballot repealing Prop. 227 and restoring "bilingual education" in California public schools. The long-dormant Language Wars may be returning to American politics, and based on the early indicators, the G.O.P. [Grand Old Party, Republicans] may have totally abandoned any support for English in the schools, with not a single Republican casting a No vote on the proposal.

Ron Unz, "California Republicans Vote to Restore 'Bilingual Education,'" *Unz Review: An Alternative Media Selection*, May 7, 2014. Copyright © 2014 Ron Unz. All rights reserved. Reproduced with permission.

Opposition to Proposition 227

Although many might be surprised by this political alignment, I am not. When I launched my "English for the Children" initiative effort in 1997 to replace California's failed system of Spanish-almost-only "bilingual education" with intensive English immersion, I sought to avoid the political partisanship that could easily taint a project touching upon delicate ethnic issues. As matters turned out, I got my wish, and our campaign was among the most bipartisan in state history, being opposed by nearly every prominent Democrat and also nearly every prominent Republican.

Requiring that English be taught in public schools was opposed by the Chairman of the state Republican Party and the Chairman of the State Democratic Party, as well as all four party leaders in the State Senate and Assembly. President Bill Clinton came out to California to campaign against us. All four candidates for governor, Democrat and Republican alike, denounced the measure and together starred in a powerful television spot urging a No vote, ranked by many as the best advertisement of that election cycle. We were opposed by every California union, every political slate, and almost every newspaper editorial board, and were outspent on advertising by a ratio of 25-to-1. But despite this daunting array of influential opponents, our initiative still passed with one of the largest political landslides of any contested measure in state history, winning over 61 percent of the vote.

During the first four years following the passage of Prop. 227, the academic performance of over a million immigrant schoolchildren taught in English roughly doubled.

As is traditional with California initiatives, our critics hoped to win in the courtroom what they had lost at the ballot box and bilingual advocates immediately sued to block the law. However, in the weeks that followed, four separate federal judges ruled in favor of Prop. 227 and the law that had passed in the June [1998] vote began to be implemented statewide as the new school year began in September. All of California's thousand-odd school districts were required to teach young immigrant children in English as soon as they started school, though some bitterly resisted and dragged their feet.

The Success of Proposition 227

The consequences were quite remarkable. Although nearly every state newspaper had editorially opposed the change in educational policy, once their journalists began visiting the schools to report the results of such a sweeping educational transformation, the many dozens of major media stories produced were uniformly glowing, with teachers, parents, and children all very happy with the change, and everyone surprised how quickly and easily the students were learning English in the classroom.

The following year, academic test scores for a million-plus immigrant students in California rose substantially, confounding naysayers and putting the story back on the front pages of the major state newspapers. And in 2000, immigrant test scores continued their rise, leading to a front-page story in the Sunday *New York Times* and major coverage in the rest of the national media. The founding president of the California Association of Bilingual Educators publicly declared that he had been wrong for thirty years and bilingual education didn't work while English immersion did work, becoming a born-again convert to "English" and appearing on *CBS News* and the *PBS Newshour* to make his case.

During the first four years following the passage of Prop. 227, the academic performance of over a million immigrant schoolchildren taught in English roughly doubled, while those school districts that stubbornly retained their bilingual education programs showed no improvement whatsoever. English-learners in English immersion classes academically outperformed their counterparts in holdover bilingual education programs in every subject, every grade level, and every year, racking up performance advantage of 80-to-0.

The political trends showed a similar trajectory, with Arizona voters passing an almost identical ballot measure by an even wider 26 point margin in November 2000 and the electorate of Massachusetts, arguably America's most liberal state, favoring "English" by a colossal 32 point landslide in 2002, incidentally putting supporter Mitt Romney in the governorship as a political side-effect. Then in 2003, Nativo Lopez, one of California's most diehard remaining backers of bilingual education, was recalled from office in Santa Ana by Latino parents outraged over his opposition to "English," losing by a 40 point margin in America's most heavily Latino immigrant major city.

With that last landslide vote over a decade ago in America's most heavily Latino immigrant city, resistance to "English" completely crumbled and bilingual education largely disappeared from schools in California and much of the rest of the country while even the term itself almost completely vanished from public discourse or media coverage.

For decades since the 1960s, denunciations of bilingual education had been a staple of conservative campaign rhetoric—the so-called "language wars"—but with the provocative educational policy having disappeared, the rhetoric eventually followed and fewer and fewer elected officials or political activists even remembered that the program had once existed. A couple of years ago, Peter Brimelow, editor of the leading anti-immigration webzine VDare.com, included a rare denunciation of bilingual education in one of his columns, but felt compelled to explain the meaning of the term, which may have become unfamiliar to his younger anti-immigrationist readers.

Meanwhile, virtually all immigrant children in California quickly and easily learned English as soon as they entered school, and no one thought the process difficult or remarkable. Whereas for decades bilingual education theorists had claimed that it took seven to ten years for a young child to learn English—a totally insane claim that was ubiquitous in our schools of education—everyone now recognized that just a few months was usually time enough, with the new goal being for Latino children to learn English in pre-school and therefore become fully English-proficient before they even entered kindergarten.

> *The replacement of bilingual education with English immersion in our public schools may rank as just about the only clear success for policies traditionally advocated by conservatives and Republicans.*

And inevitably, the Prop. 227 educational revolution has produced a generation of mostly bilingual young adults. After all, a large fraction of California Latinos are raised in Spanish-speaking households, and learn that language as children. Meanwhile, they now learn to read and write and speak mainstream English as soon as they enter school, while often continuing to speak Spanish at home with their parents and other family members. Thus, millions of younger Californians have ended up with complete fluency in both languages, effortlessly switching between the two, as I have personally often noticed in Palo Alto, a town in which perhaps half the ordinary daily workers are Hispanic in origin.

Little Attention to the Revolution

One reason this educational revolution has attracted so little ongoing attention is that it merely served to align instructional curriculum with overwhelming popular sentiment. Even a decade or more ago, while the policy was still under sharp political dispute, numerous state and national surveys had indicated that nearly 80% of all Americans supported having all public school instruction conducted in English, with these massive supermajorities cutting across all ideological, political, ethnic, and geographical lines, and support among immigrant Hispanics being especially strong. Indeed, I am not aware of any contentious policy issue whose backing was so totally uniform and overwhelming.

But politics abhors a vacuum and although almost everyone else has forgotten the topic of bilingual education over the last dozen years, the small number of bilingual zealots have remained just as committed as ever to their failed dogma. I doubt that there ever numbered more than just a few hundred hardcore bilingual activist supporters among California's population of over thirty million, but their years of unopposed private lobbying and spurious academic research have now borne fruit. California politicians are hardly deep thinkers and term limits ensured that few of them had been prominent in public life during the late 1990s. Hence the 8-to-0 committee vote to reestablish bilingual education in California.

In reviewing the last twenty years of domestic policy battles in America, the replacement of bilingual education with English immersion in our public schools may rank as just about the only clear success for policies traditionally advocated by conservatives and Republicans—at least no other obvious example comes to mind. Meanwhile, the disastrous political choices made by California Republicans during the 1990s have placed what was once the most powerful Republican state party in America on the very edge of irrelevance and a descent into minor-party status.

For California Republicans to back the restoration of failed bilingual education programs would probably mark the final nail in their coffin, and rightfully so.

7

Bilingual Education Using Native Language Is Best for Immigrants

Daniel A. Domenech

Daniel A. Domenech is the executive director of the American Association of School Administrators.

Bilingual education in New York has become devalued over the years, despite a growing population of non-English-speaking immigrant children. Opposition to bilingual education is unreasonable when so many of these children lack basic literacy in their native tongue.

One of my responsibilities in my first administrative job was to develop and direct a bilingual education program for the Nassau County Board of Cooperative Educational Services [BOCES] in New York. In 1972, I submitted an application for federal funding under what then was known as the Bilingual Education Act, or Title VII of the Elementary and Secondary Education Act.

Bilingual Education in New York

The BOCES system is an educational service agency providing for the needs of the component districts in its region, and the Nassau BOCES, the largest in the state, serves 56 school districts on Long Island.

Daniel A. Domenech, "The Unfortunate Devolution of Bilingual Instruction," *School Administrator*, vol. 68, no. 5, May 2011. Copyright © 2011 American Association of School Administrators. All rights reserved. Reproduced with permission.

To my delight, the proposal was funded, and we organized the programs. We selected communities in Nassau County, a suburb of New York City with a high concentration of non-English-speaking students. We offered instruction in three languages—Spanish, Italian and Portuguese—and Hempstead, Long Beach, Westbury, Mineola and Glen Cove were among the first communities served.

Our model created multiaged classrooms in the highest impacted schools and provided a trained bilingual teacher and aide. In those days, not many schools of education provided bilingual education training, so one of our first activities was to recruit teachers who were bilingual in a target language and train them to be effective bilingual educators. One of my first trainers was Betty Molina Morgan, who recently finished her term as National Superintendent of the Year.

Because of the Aspira Consent Decree, a court ruling mandating bilingual education, the city of New York took the lead in developing bilingual programs in the state. Although the consent decree did not require the rest of the state to provide bilingual programs, the Title VII funds made it possible for many suburban areas to create new ways to serve the needs of their growing populations of English language learners.

If the devaluation of bilingual education was supposed to result in significant academic gains, then the strategy has failed miserably.

Hernan LaFontaine was the director of bilingual programs in New York City at the time. He later went on to become superintendent in Hartford, Conn., and most recently worked with the Connecticut Association of Public School Superintendents. LaFontaine helped the rest of us in the state as we implemented our own programs. Our collaboration would lead eventually to the founding of the New York State Association for Bilingual Education. I am proud to have been its first president.

A Devaluation Period

Since those days, bilingual education seems to have devolved rather than evolved. There is no longer a Title VII to fund bilingual programs. There isn't even a bilingual office in the U.S. Department of Education. States like California and Massachusetts, in essence, have banned bilingual instruction.

A huge demographic shift has taken hold since the 1970s. Back then, only 6 percent of the school-age population was Hispanic. Today, at 19 percent, they are the largest minority group in our schools. If the devaluation of bilingual education was supposed to result in significant academic gains, then the strategy has failed miserably.

At a time when there is a significant emphasis on closing the achievement gap, reducing the dropout rate and increasing the percentage of students graduating from high school, Hispanics are at the short end of the stick in every category. Out of 100 Hispanic 9th graders, only 53 will graduate from high school. Twenty-seven will go on to college, but only 10 of them will graduate.

Along with African-American students, 33 percent of Hispanic students, many of them English language learners, make up the majority of the student population at so-called dropout factories. In discussions focusing on turning around those schools, bilingual education should be included as a strategy that can make a difference for those students.

Unreasonable Opposition

I find it difficult to understand why anyone would oppose teaching students in the language they best understand. I accept that it might be impossible to do so in areas where bilingual teachers are not available. I would be the last person to debate the critical importance of being functionally literate in the English language.

I came to the United States as a 9-year-old immigrant from my native Cuba. Total immersion worked for me. I was placed in a boarding school in Tarrytown, N.Y., where no one spoke Spanish. It was sink or swim, and I swam. Within three months, I could speak and understand enough English to get by. But I came to this country as a literate 5th grader with a solid foundation on which to build.

However, that is not the case today for the majority of our immigrant students, who come to us often illiterate in their native language and without a solid foundation to build on. More than 40 years of research in second-language acquisition in this country affirm the effectiveness of using the native language to learn higher-level concepts while learning the English language. And maintaining a child's native language would be so much more effective than trying to teach them a "foreign" language at the secondary level.

My experiences tell me the issue has less to do with research and pedagogy and perhaps more to do with prejudice and politics. If we are to be competitive in this global economy, if we are to lead the world in the percentage of our population with college degrees, then we cannot afford to do anything less in the classroom than what research and pedagogy indicate is appropriate.

8

Language Immersion Is Better than Bilingual Education for Immigrants

Linda Chavez

Linda Chavez is chairman of the Center for Equal Opportunity, a nonprofit public policy research organization, and a syndicated columnist.

Despite the success of English immersion programs, there are attempts to reinstate bilingual education in California. Such a move would be bad for immigrant children and bad for the future of immigration reform, since opponents of immigration fear its threat to the English language in the United States.

California is home to the largest population of limited English-speaking students in the nation, mostly immigrants and children of immigrants from Latin America and Asia. If these children are to succeed in the United States, they must learn English—the question is how best to accomplish that aim. In 1998, after decades of failing such students, Californians voted to replace so-called bilingual education, which in practice taught children primarily in their native language, with English immersion programs.

The Success of English Immersion

By all measures, the shift away from native-language instruction toward English immersion was a success. Not only did kids learn English more quickly, but their reading scores im-

Linda Chavez, "Being Pro-English Is Also Pro-Immigrant," *Townhall*, June 6, 2014. Copyright © 2014 Creators Syndicate. All rights reserved. By permission of Linda Chavez and Creators Syndicate, Inc.

proved, as well, doubling in the first four years after bilingual education was banned. So why are California legislators now trying to reverse course and lift the ban on bilingual education? The move seems primarily aimed at appeasing a powerful bilingual education lobby. If bilingual educators succeed, it will be at the expense not only of the children they claim to want to help, but also of the future of immigration reform.

The proponents of reinstating bilingual education in California seem far more interested in expanding the use of Spanish in American life than they do in helping children learn English.

Scratch the surface of arguments against immigration, and you'll quickly find the suspicion that immigrants, especially Latinos, will transform America and American culture. And the No. 1 fear that comes up is language. I can't count the times I've heard the charge that today's immigrants are different from their counterparts from Europe in the early 20th century. Latino immigrants, critics claim, "refuse" to learn English. Never mind that the evidence overwhelmingly demonstrates that Latinos are following in the footsteps of every other group that has come to America speaking a language other than English, not only becoming fluent in the second generation, but also largely losing the ability to speak Spanish by the third generation.

The perception stems from two factors: First, the huge influx of new immigrants from Latin America over the past several decades means we have a large population of Spanish speakers, some 37 million. Second, this population has created a market for goods and services offered in Spanish. "Press 1 for English" is the result of capitalism responding to this opportunity to reach customers. And for more than 40 years, government policy has encouraged the trend by mandating bilingual services in everything from education and social services to voting. I've spent a career fighting such mandates, especially in voting, but the fact is the mandates existed even before the large expansion of Spanish-speaking immigrants.

The Proponents of Bilingual Education

The proponents of reinstating bilingual education in California seem far more interested in expanding the use of Spanish in American life than they do in helping children learn English. And that's a problem, especially for those who want to encourage a change in our immigration laws that would make it easier for people to come here legally. Anti-immigration groups couldn't find a more effective argument in favor of restricting immigration than claiming the United States will soon require everyone to know Spanish, as well as English. Ironically, some of the most virulently racist groups out there would happily force all Latino kids into bilingual classes.

As Ron Unz, the man who managed to pass the 1998 California ballot initiative banning bilingual education, pointed out recently, white nationalists Richard Spencer and Jared Taylor both have endorsed bilingual education. Spencer recently tweeted, "I oppose forcing Hispanic children to learn English," which drew widespread approval from his followers, whose views were succinctly summed up by one respondent: "Long term: a bunch of mestizos learning English will only dumbdown and sully English." Their hope is that bilingual education will lead to the de-facto segregation of Latino kids.

But some nine out of 10 Latinos believe it is imperative for Latinos to learn English. And immigrants are especially eager for their children to learn the language that will enable them to build a better future for themselves. Indeed, it was immigrant parents who pushed hardest for eliminating failing bilingual programs in California in 1998.

Craven politicians of both parties—Republican legislators joined with Democrats to push the repeal of English immersion through committee—will do great harm if they return

California to the bad old days when kids who desperately needed and wanted to learn English were stuck in classrooms where they were denied that opportunity. Thankfully, the proposed repeal must still go before California voters. Let's hope voters have more sense and compassion than their elected leaders.

9

How Union City Is Shifting the Arc of Immigrant Kids' Lives

David L. Kirp

David L. Kirp is the James D. Marver professor in the Goldman School of Public Policy at the University of California, Berkeley, and author of Improbable Scholars: The Rebirth of a Great American School System *and a* Strategy for America's Schools, *from which this article has been adapted.*

A New Jersey school's bilingual program illustrates what works best for older immigrant children. Instead of placing them directly into all-English classes, the school gradually transitions them from bilingual education to English-only, ensuring they have the skills to succeed.

Most school districts do a rotten job of educating immigrant youngsters. Routinely, they are shunted to poorly funded, overcrowded and understaffed schools, where teacher turnover is high and expectations low. They leave school prepared only for the brawn-work and domestic labor that no one else will touch.

A Bright Spot for Urban Education

Union City, New Jersey, four miles and light years from Times Square [New York City], has turned this narrative of failure on its head by bringing students like these into the education

David L. Kirp, "How Union City Is Shifting the Arc of Immigrant Kids' Lives," *Nation*, April 8, 2013. © 2013 The Nation Company, LLC. All rights reserved. Used by permission and protected by the Copyright Laws of the United States. The printing, copying, redistribution, or retransmission of this Content without express written permission is prohibited mainstream. The city makes an unlikely poster child for urban education. It's one of America's poorest and most crowded municipalities, with an unemployment rate nearly 50 percent higher than the national average. The population is overwhelmingly Latino, and it's estimated that a quarter of the residents are undocumented—"*sin papeles*" [without papers] as they say. Three-quarters of the students are growing up in homes where Spanish is the language at the dining table and telenovelas, not reality shows, are the TV staple.

In other cities with similar demographics, many of these students would drop out or flunk out. In years past, that was the case in Union City. But now the situation is completely reversed.

Here's the headline: scores on the high-stakes reading and math tests approximate the statewide average. What's even more impressive, in 2011, *90 percent of the students graduated— that's more than 10 percent higher than the national average— and nearly 75 percent enrolled in college.* Step by step, from preschool through high school, Union City has devised a strategy that any school district can use.

Preschool plays a pivotal part in Union City's success. Iconic field studies have shown the powerful life-long impact of good early education. "Skill begets skill"—that's how Nobel Prize-winning economist James Heckman sums up the research.

In Union City . . . immigrant kids are eased into English, lesson by lesson and student by student.

Outside evaluators give Union City's early education program high marks for the education it delivers. Seeing is believing.

In Suzy Rojas's class, art plasters the walls, plants hang from the ceiling, and in every niche there's something to seize a child's imagination. Angel, Victor and Rodrigo are peering at insects through a microscope, and they're happy to explain to me what they're seeing. "Are these all insects?" Suzy wonders aloud. "How do you know?" "That one has eight legs," Victor responds, "and that means it's not an insect." Then Suzy brings over a prism. "What do you see when you look through it?" she asks, and Rodrigo looks up to say that he can't tell them apart, that they look like leaves. "Why do you think so?" The youngsters have already learned about lenses, and she tells them that the prism is a special kind of lens.

When Victor and Rodrigo start fighting over who gets the next look at the lens, Suzy tells them to "use your words." That's familiar teacher-talk, but then she adds a twist. "What can we do"—we, not you: the boys think about it. "How about adding another container for insects—that way you can all take turns."

"I think of preschool as the Magic Kingdom," says Adriana Birne, who runs the district's early education program. "Whatever is happening in the rest of these children's lives, this is a wonderful place to be." Even the kids who come to preschool without knowing a word of English are primed for kindergarten.

The Challenges for Older Immigrants

Learning America goes most smoothly for youngsters who cross the border when they are very young, because they have the blessing of time to grasp English in a bosomy setting. Three or four years later they're truly bilingual, and they're doing as well as kids born in the United States. But the older they are when they come to the US the greater the test they pose.

The education of a new arrival varies with how much English they know as well as their academic aptitude. Though that might sound obvious, it's the decided exception. In several states, California and Arizona among them, bilingual education has been abolished, politics triumphing over pedagogy. Elsewhere, youngsters in the throes of mastering a new tongue go straight from a bilingual class to an English-only class. There, the students have been speaking English all their lives and the teacher hasn't been trained to address their particular needs. Not surprisingly, these youngsters often flounder. In Union City, by contrast, immigrant kids are eased into English, lesson by lesson and student by student.

> Alina Bossbaly, who teaches third grade, is constantly in motion, whirling like a ballerina from one small group of students to another, one youngster to another, giving hugs and tousling hair, switching languages in midsentence, English to Spanish and back again, with the occasional bit of Spanglish tossed into the linguistic pot. "*Mi corazon* [my heart]," she murmurs, "*mi amor* [my love]." When she reads aloud to the class, shifting between the Spanish and English translations, she acts out all the parts, her expressions as evocative as a mime's.
>
> At the start of the year, half of Alina's youngsters were being taught entirely in Spanish, but two months later some of them have begun to read in English. They've been prepared for that shift—from day one they have been hearing lots of English spoken in the room, and in their small groups they've been playing a game with blocks that teaches them how to construct English words. Alina won't push these kids, for she wants to make sure they've honed their Spanish before they read and write entirely in English. "There aren't many children in this country who know two languages," she reminds them. "It's a real advantage."

Students who arrive as teenagers, about a sixth of the high school population, have the hardest time making the grade. Many of them have spent only a few years in school before coming to the US, and they read and write Spanish at a grade school level. They know nothing about paragraphs or punctuation, fractions or photosynthesis, George Washington or Simon Bolivar [military leader who liberated Latin America from Spanish control]. A high school diploma marks the first step on the path to a decent life—high school graduates earn 25 percent more than dropouts—but to graduate, and maybe continue on to college, these youngsters must squeeze half a lifetime of school into three or four years. Surprisingly, many of them do just that.

[Union City High School] has thought through the pathway to graduation. . . . They also get these kids into mainstream life of the school, sports and after-school activities as well as academics.

A Pathway to Graduation

The education of teenage newcomers with the shakiest skills starts, in Union City, with a "port of entry" class. Students' progress is regularly monitored, and those who do well move swiftly into English as a Second Language courses, then into an English class designed to prepare them for English-only instruction. By the time they're seniors they'll have disappeared into the general population.

Laura Maczuzak, who is introducing a class of eleven port of entry students to the rudiments of English, is working her way through the words that describe different facial features. "What is hair?—show me. Does anyone in the class have red hair? How about a moustache? Dimples? I'm the only one with wrinkles," she jokes. When she asks who has a scar, every hand pops up—in this class, everyone bears a scar on his face.

Later, these teens will take Sophie Karanikopolos's English class, one of the new, almost-mainstream classes. This is the last time they'll be treated specially because they are native Spanish-speakers; next semester they'll be in a regular English class. It's October, which Sophie, mindful of her students' *True Blood* fixation, has turned into Gothic romance month, and the students are reading Edgar Allan Poe's "Telltale Heart" and "The Pit and the Pendulum." A year earlier, in an English as a Second Language class, they would have parsed the text line by line to check for comprehension. Here they are dissecting Poe's use of suspense, and unless you'd been told, you would never suspect that this isn't a garden-variety English class.

Sophie pushes her students to "think college." She and her colleagues prep them for the SAT [college admission exam], which they are all expected to take, and help them fill out their college applications. "I tell my students 'if college is what you want, then we'll get you there.' Undocumented kids too—even though they'll have a very hard time getting scholarships or loans, I say that 'if you have the motivation we'll figure out a way to deal with the money issues.'"

"The kids love you unconditionally," she adds. "They're interested in learning, and they have so much respect and admiration."

The Center for Applied Linguistics in Washington, DC, has singled out these initiatives as among the nation's best. At the Center, Deborah Short, who conducted the research, tells me that Union City High "has created a culture that respects differences and promotes learning. The school expects its students to do well and it gives them lots of support."

"What's crucial," she adds, "is that the high school has thought through the pathway to graduation. Most places have a set view of what all students take in a particular grade. They put students into empty desks rather than determining who is the right teacher and what is the best plan for each student. They also get these kids into mainstream life of the school, sports and after-school activities as well as academics."

The American Dream Come True

This June [2013], 600 seniors will walk across the stage, shake the principal's hand and receive their diplomas. Two of the top ten graduates came to the US just four years ago, and when they arrived in Union City they knew no English.

As you might expect, this school system does well by all its students, not just the newcomers. In a 2012 study of 22,000 high schools, the American Institutes of Research rated Union City High among the top 20 percent and a few years back the district passed a soup-to-nuts state review with flying colors, the only urban school system to do so. The fact that Union City is handsomely funded, thanks to a New Jersey court ruling that funnels extra state dollars to the poorest districts, makes a considerable difference. But many districts that are just as well supported haven't done nearly as well academically.

Union City hasn't bottled a magic elixir. Quite the contrary, it has stuck with the tried-and-true, tweaking its program as needed but keeping its basic strategy, constructing a system of supports, like the finely granulated program for newcomers which reaches from preschool to high school. That's the takeaway for school districts nationwide as they ponder how to give immigrant kids the education they deserve.

> It's standing room only for the 2011 graduation ceremony. Amid the round of valedictory addresses, a senior named Hamlet Diaz steals the show. Hamlet, a blind student, knew no English when he came to Union City from the Dominican Republic as a boy. He speaks movingly about how he learned to read and write in Braille—how he was able, with lots of help along the way, to make it. The superintendent is crying, the principal is sobbing. Massive linemen from the football team, sitting shoulder to shoulder, have tears in their eyes. You can't find a dry eye in the house.

Silvia Abbato, now the assistant superintendent, was Hamlet's elementary school principal. "We're working on getting him into college," she tells me. "It's not easy because [he's undocumented], but we'll figure it out."

That's the American dream come true—and there's no reason why it shouldn't be within reach of every kid in America.

10

Bilingual Education Must Succeed at Helping Students Learn English

Trevon Milliard

Trevon Milliard is a K-12 education reporter at the Las Vegas Review-Journal.

Despite the growing number of English-language learners (ELLs) in the United States, teachers do not feel qualified to effectively teach them. Although schools may want students to retain their native language, the goal must be to teach proficiency in English.

More than 5.3 million American public school students would struggle to understand this sentence.

A Lack of Training

These students need to be taught the English language in addition to the usual material in math, science, and social studies. This presents a monumental challenge for educators nationwide, according to Patricia Gandara, a UCLA [University of California, Los Angeles] education professor whom President Barack Obama appointed to the Commission on Educational Excellence for Hispanics. She is also co-director of the Civil Rights Project at the University of California, Los Angeles.

Trevon Milliard, "Millions of American Students Need to Learn English," *Atlantic*, December 19, 2013. Copyright © 2013 The Atlantic Media Co., as first published in The Atlantic Magazine. All rights reserved. Distributed by Tribune Content Agency, LLC. Reproduced by permission.

Speaking at the Education Writers Association's [EWA] National Seminar, held in May [2013] at Stanford University, Gandara referenced a nationwide survey given to teachers already trained for the growing number of English-language learners, commonly called ELLs.

"In the words of teachers themselves, they don't feel qualified," Gandara said.

About 40 percent of American teachers have ELL students in their classrooms, but only a third of these teachers have training for them. However, this training usually amounts to just four hours over five years, said Gandara on Saturday, laying the ground for a panel of ELL experts and teachers discussing why intensive efforts have failed to close the gaps of ELL students.

Schools can't agree on whether to adopt bilingual education or just teaching English, treating native languages as a "crutch."

"This is really difficult to do," said Gandara, quoting a bilingual teacher who still struggles to keep ELL students on track despite speaking Spanish, the native language of three-fourths of America's ELL students.

Ashley Bessire teaches at a charter school that has managed success despite an enrollment that's 82 percent ELL students. The approach of her Austin [Texas] school, KIPP Comunidad, is "one face one language." Each teacher sticks to one language in all their instruction, meaning students transition from Spanish to English-speaking classrooms throughout the day. And teachers of different languages overlap material. An English-based writing teacher might ask students to write about what they learned in their Spanish-based science course, Bessire told the EWA audience.

Developing Proficiency in English

The school wants students to know their native language as well as English, but the goal is for students to actually score higher in comprehension of their native language than English, she said.

Kenji Hakuta, a Stanford University education professor and co-chair of the Understanding Language initiative, was quick to point out that KIPP's dual-language approach—although effective—wouldn't be allowed in other states or, in many cases, outside charter schools. Schools can't agree on whether to adopt bilingual education or just teaching English, treating native languages as a "crutch," said Hakuta, who joined Gandara and Bessire on the panel.

"We've been at this since Congress passed the 1968 Bilingual Education Act," he said.

But the newly implemented Common Core Standards will force schools to do something Bessire and other KIPP teachers already do, Hakuta said. Under the standards, students aren't allowed to just produce an answer but must explain how they came to that answer, integrating language at all times.

Currently, students may go through an entire school day without speaking a word of English, noted the panel's moderator, Kathryn Baron of *EdSource Today*. If not verbally approached throughout the day, Common Core would force students to do it in writing.

Whether Common Core alone would make a difference remains to be seen, but schools need to draw down their increasing number of ELL students from where it stands at 5.3 million, Hakuta said. To shed their label, ELL students must become proficient in English.

"Ultimately, we need to put Humpty Dumpty back together again," said Hakuta, noting that some research suggests this takes five years.

11

Bilingual Education Should Support Heritage Language Literacy

Olga Kagan

Olga Kagan is a professor in the University of California, Los Angeles' Department of Slavic, East European, and Eurasian Languages and Cultures and the director of the National Heritage Language Resource Center.

Although it should not come at the expense of learning English, there is a great opportunity in supporting students in retaining their heritage language—the native language of their parents that they use at home—and developing bilingual literacy. Because of its multilingual nature, Los Angeles is an ideal place to test heritage language programs in the schools.

Many students in Los Angeles, from kindergarten through college, speak a language other than English because they grew up hearing it. They are "heritage speakers," the children of immigrants who communicate at home in their parents' native language. Yet many of these students have no literacy in the language they speak. And that is a problem.

The Population of Heritage Speakers

Although heritage speakers have a good head start, they need classes targeted to their needs if they are to be truly bilingual. The urban landscape of Los Angeles is multilingual—and an

Olga Kagan, "Schools Should Help the Children of Immigrants Become Truly Bilingual," *Los Angeles Times*, December 21, 2014. Copyright © 2014 Olga Kagan. All rights reserved. Reproduced with permission.

ideal place to implement a far-reaching policy devoted to maintaining and developing the skills of heritage speakers.

According to a survey conducted by the Census Bureau, the number of people in the U.S. who speak a language other than English is almost 21%. In California it's more than double that, with almost 44% of residents speaking a language other than English at home. In Los Angeles County, that figure climbs to almost 57%.

A significant percentage of the more than 12 million residents in the metropolitan Los Angeles region speak a language other than English at home. While about 4.4 million are Spanish speakers, the survey found that other languages are amply represented. About 415,000 speak Chinese, 272,000 Tagalog and 258,000 Korean. Another 103,000 speak Persian and 55,000 Russian.

We need to embrace and advance homegrown bilingualism, but that can happen only if we offer these languages in our educational system.

Although Spanish is offered at all public high schools, most of the other languages are taught at only a handful of schools. Russian is taught at one high school, and several languages, such as Tagalog and Persian, are not taught at all, according to my research.

A Missed Opportunity

By not teaching the languages that many students often only half-know, we are missing an opportunity to expand the number of Americans completely comfortable with other languages and cultures—a tremendous asset in today's increasingly globalized world. This loss of potential fluent speakers has long-term consequences for national security (remember the lack of Arabic speakers after 9/11?), business (it's not all about English anymore), family relations (what if parents don't speak English well, and children don't speak the home language well?) and social services (professionals speaking multiple languages are in high demand).

We need to embrace and advance homegrown bilingualism, but that can happen only if we offer these languages in our educational system. And, of course, it should not be done at the expense of learning English, which remains the sine qua non [something essential] to function in the world.

A recent survey conducted by the National Heritage Language Resource Center at UCLA [University of California, Los Angeles] showed that many college students would elect to formally study their home language to gain literacy, discover more about their heritage culture and linguistic roots, and communicate better with relatives. That can happen only if the language is offered as part of a curriculum for heritage speakers that takes their existing proficiencies into account. They won't be served well by a beginning language class because they arrive with considerable skills—and a beginning class assumes zero knowledge.

The Roadblocks for Heritage-Language Programs

A smattering of schools offer instruction in languages spoken in their local communities. For example, Chinese is offered in Alhambra, Armenian in Glendale, Khmer in Long Beach and Vietnamese in Orange County. Some offer programs for heritage students. For example, Chinese, Korean and Arabic are taught as part of a heritage-language curriculum at Granada Hills Charter High School. Most schools do not teach the languages of their local communities, and if they do, they don't differentiate between the curriculum for foreign-language and heritage-language learners.

While Vietnamese immigrants first settled the city of Westminster in the mid-1970s, Westminster High did not offer its first Vietnamese language course until 1999. Now Vietnamese is taught in several schools in the Garden Grove School District, and there are plans to expand the curriculum to more schools.

Schools that want to introduce a local heritage-language program must overcome multiple roadblocks: Finding credentialed teachers of less-commonly taught languages and ensuring the teachers know how to teach heritage-language learners. Schools of education, university language departments and school districts need to come together to prepare teachers to implement a curriculum that takes students' home-based competencies into account and allows them to progress at a faster rate.

Language skills need be nurtured at home—and in the classroom. The dozens of languages spoken in Los Angeles make it the ideal place to lead the charge.

12

Bilingual Education Is a Promising Solution in Former Colonies

Corinne Brion

Corinne Brion is a doctoral student in educational leadership at the University of California, San Diego, and has taught French as a second language for two decades.

The imposition of French in Burkina Faso during colonial times has left much of the population unable to participate in education and society. A better model to monolingual French schools is a transitional model that takes five years of bilingual education to help students acquire French.

In one of the world's poorest countries, a model of bilingual education is emerging that could have a substantial effect on the nation. Landlocked, sub-Saharan Burkina Faso has battled high illiteracy and high dropout rates since gaining independence from France in 1960. Scholars say the problem stems from the lack of culturally appropriate education, and some have suggested bilingual education as part of a solution. To that extent, the Burkinabe government and local nongovernmental organizations have started a program, Bilingual Indigenous Community Education, which aims to instruct students in both their native tongue and the country's French national language.

Corinne Brion, "Two Languages are Better Than One." *Phi Delta Kappan*, Vol 96 (3) pp. 70–72. Copyright © 2014 by Phi Delta Kappa International. Reprinted by permission of SAGE Publications, Inc.

Language in Burkina Faso

A brief history and overview of the region may help explain why. Burkina Faso borders Mali to the north, Niger to the northeast, and Ghana and Cote d'Ivoire to the south. Some 16 million people are spread over 105,000 square miles of dry land. Yet the country relies heavily on agriculture, with 77% of the population living in rural areas. More than half the population is under 15 years old. Women bear an average of 6.2 children, and life expectancy is 51 years.

The Burkinabe progressively lost much of their individual and collective identities, preventing them from taking the initiative to change their educational systems.

The Anglo-French Convention of 1898 ended the fighting between Britain and France and created new borders between their colonies. In 1919, the French further divided their area of land, separating Upper Volta from French Sudan and then further dismantled and divided this colony in 1932. By 1947, the French restored Upper Volta as a separate territory in French West Africa. In 1960, the nation gained its independence from France. It was renamed Burkina Faso in 1984, taking a word from each of the country's two major native languages, Moore and Dioula. (Burkina is "men of integrity" in Moore; Faso in Dioula means "fatherland.")

These geographical and historical summaries are significant because of their effect on the educational system. Burkina Faso has always lacked resources such as water, minerals, fertile soil, oil, and gas. Thus, during colonization, the French invested mainly in Dakar, Senegal, because it was not only more easily accessible but more profitable. As a result, Burkina Faso failed to develop critical infrastructures and fell behind in many areas, including education. The country has a literacy rate of only 46%, and a youth unemployment rate around 43%. The country has struggled to catch up with the rest of the continent; the first university in the capital city, Ouaga-dougou, was not established until 1974.

The Imposition of French

The colonial experience was traumatic in many ways. The French imposed their language as the exclusive means of instruction, although there are 59 native languages in Burkina Faso, and 90% of the population speak just 14 of them. The Burkinabe progressively lost much of their individual and collective identities, preventing them from taking the initiative to change their educational systems.

While a report by the French Ministry of Foreign Affairs suggests that education scores are improving overall, the achievement rate of primary education has some critical gaps.

This reveals a gender discrepancy, with boys scoring more than 10 points higher than girls. Girls often miss school because they are asked to stay home to help with chores, are promised in marriage at a young age, or are pregnant. Culturally, girls don't tend to return to school regularly once they have a family. The second discrepancy is the significant difference between city and rural children. Rural children often don't have as many resources as students in cities, they have less-qualified teachers, and often their parents are unable to help with their schoolwork.

Currently monolingual schools—in which the colonial language, French, is used as the language of instruction—remain the dominant model in the Burkinabe education system. This has seriously hindered Burkina Faso's growth and development.

As the official language of Burkina Faso, French is used not only in monolingual schools but also in media, government offices, courts, and diplomacy. Street signs and the main newspapers are published in French. Given these realities,

French tends to be seen as the language of development and hope, not only by the elite but also by the Burkinabe people in general.

But only 10% to 15% of the populace speak or understand French. Children of the country's elite speak French and successfully attend monolingual schools; they're the only ones with access to additional resources and tutoring. This means most children are expected to sit quietly at schools day after day, without being able to understand what is being taught. Some students become depressed and sick because they feel ashamed when they're unable to participate in lessons. Additionally, corporal punishment is often used when students speak their native tongue, exacerbating their feeling of not fitting in the class. Since the exam administered at the end of primary school also is in French, children who come from families with limited means either fail or quit school.

Bilingual education trains children to enjoy learning and helps them become independent and self-sufficient.

A Transitional Model

Burkina Faso officially implemented bilingual education in 1994 with the opening of two schools. In 1996, a Burkinabe law made it acceptable to use national languages in formal schools, which are public schools that receive funding, staffing, and materials from the government. The government and l'Oeuvre Suisse d'entraide Ouvriere (OSEO, now known as SOLIDAR) have worked collaboratively to promote bilingual education throughout the country. SOLIDAR is a nongovernmental organization that works on behalf of less fortunate people in nations across the globe. So far, there are 204 bilingual public schools in 28 out of the 45 provinces, using eight national languages. Since 2008, the nation has opened an average of 20 bilingual schools per year, with 45 opened during the 2013 school year. In addition, there are 100 requests from diverse parent-teacher associations to convert monolingual schools into bilingual programs.

Bilingual education in formal primary settings follows the transitional model. Students spend their first year of school learning 90% in their native tongue and 10% in French. Second-year students learn in their native tongue 75% to 80% of the time and the remainder in French. In their third year, students are educated in both languages in equal amounts, preparing them for the fourth year when they transition to 20% of the time in the national language and 80% in French. This allows them to finish primary school at 90% of French instruction and the remainder in their local language. At the end of 5th grade, the students take their first national exam in French, le Certificat d'Etude Primaire (CEP).

The bilingual school curriculum is identical to that of the monolingual French schools except that it has added cultural and agricultural activities. These are intended to provide the students with skills they will need to be self-sufficient. Another significant difference is that bilingual schools not only encourage parent participation but consider it essential for success. Parents teach cultural modules that include songs and dances, as well as practical economical skills, such as basket weaving, how to seed a field, and how to raise cattle. In bilingual classes, children participate and even take leadership roles. This seems to boost class attendance, particularly among girls. In sum, bilingual education trains children to enjoy learning and helps them become independent and self-sufficient, which benefits their families, community, and the country as a whole.

This new model of education must overcome several challenges if it is to continue to grow throughout the country and perhaps the continent. First, bilingual education must win the battle against the elite who oppose it for fear of losing ground. By preserving French as the main language of instruction, the elite believe their children will have an easier time getting administrative jobs. Another challenge to this model is the cost of developing materials in several native languages. Finally, most parents still believe that unless their children learn French fluently by having it as the sole language of instruction, they will be at a disadvantage. However, many linguists have proven that learning initially in a language that students understand enhances the learning of other languages later. This transitional model does not seek to erase French completely, but to introduce it as a second language later.

The Bilingual Indigenous Community Education program enables children to learn, helps keep them motivated, teaches them practical skills, and slowly integrates French into the curriculum once they are cognitively ready for it. In addition, this model allows more girls to attend school and enables parents to participate in their children's education. Given its initial positive results, this model may well be the solution for Burkina Faso and other former colonies to grow in healthy ways and to reach their full economic, social, and cultural potential.

13

There Are Benefits to the Brain from Growing Up Bilingual

Judy Willis

Judy Willis is a board-certified neurologist and middle school teacher.

Brain research finds that bilingualism results in benefits to the prefrontal cortex activity networks. Such research should encourage parents to retain native language use at home and correct the mistaken assumption that the brain is overwhelmed by the exposure to two languages during its development.

Recent studies of children who grow up in bilingual settings reveal advantages over single language children, including both increased attentive focus and cognition. The findings correlate with prefrontal cortex brain activity networks, which direct the highest levels of thinking and awareness.

The Benefits of Biligualism

Compared to monolinguals, the studied bilingual children, who had had five to ten years of bilingual exposure, averaged higher scores in cognitive performance on tests and had greater attention focus, distraction resistance, decision-making, judgment and responsiveness to feedback. The correlated neuroimaging (fMRI [functional magnetic resonance imaging]

Judy Willis, "Bilingual Brains—Smarter & Faster," *Psychology Today*, November 22, 2012. Copyright © 2012 Dr. Judy Willis. All rights reserved. Reproduced with permission.

scans) of these children revealed greater activity in the prefrontal cortex networks directing these and other executive functions.

This increased executive function activation in the brains of children in bilingual settings extends beyond the translation of language intake and output. The powerful implications of the new research are about brainpower enhanced by growing up bilingual.

The networks that appear more active in the brains of bilingual children are part of the brain's CEO [chief executive officer, in this case, the prefrontal cortex] networks, called executive functions. These are a constellation of cognitive abilities that support goal-oriented behavior including directing attentive focus, prioritizing, planning, self-monitoring, inhibitory control, judgment, working memory (maintenance and manipulation of information), and analysis.

[Researchers] suggest the bilingual brain is highly engaged in the cognitive challenge of evaluating between the two competing language systems.

It is not during the first months or even years of life that the brain undergoes its greatest changes with regard to cognition. These neural networks of executive functions are the last regions of the brain to "mature" as recognized by the pruning of unused circuits and the myelination of the most active networks that as they become stronger and more efficient.

Executive functions such as selective attentive focus and the ability to block out distraction are typically minimally developed in childhood. These functions gradually become stronger throughout the years of prefrontal cortex maturation into the mid twenties. It is with regard to these executive functions that research about the "bilingual brain" is particularly exciting.

Research on Bilingual Brains

This aspect of bilingual research has focused on bilingual up-bringing with one language spoken at home that is not the same as the dominant language of the country. The interpretations of researchers, such as Ellen Bialystok who compared responses of 6-year olds from bilingual and monolingual homes, suggest the bilingual brain is highly engaged in the cognitive challenge of evaluating between the two competing language systems. This requires executive function attention selecting and focusing on the language being used while intentionally inhibiting the activity of the competing language system.

Too often, social pressures and mistaken beliefs often limit children benefiting from the bilingual brain booster.

When bilingual brains evaluate language, control and storage networks of both their languages are active and available. This ongoing processing, that seems instantaneous, is not reflexive or unconscious. It requires deliberate focus of attention on specific input and withholding of focus from simultaneous distracting input to analyze the language being used. Their brains need to evaluate and determine not only the meaning of words, but also which patterns of sentence structure and grammar apply and recognize nuances of pronunciation unique to the language of focus.

Bialystok describes this massive activity as exercising the executive functions early in bilinguals at work to decipher these multiple codes within each language. These control networks make choices, such as which memory storage circuits are the language-correct ones to activate from which to select the correct word, syntax, and pronunciation. The choices are demanding of a CEO that can simultaneously direct where ongoing new input is sent for successful evaluation and activate the correct language storage banks to use for response.

These executive functions simultaneously coordinate the evaluation of the content of the messages and direct the response to that information.

One of the most significant implications of the bilingual research is the recognition that even very young children's executive functions appear responsive to exercise which strengthens them for future use. An example from the research is these children's higher scores on cognitive testing.

Mistaken Parental Beliefs

This incoming research supports encouraging parents to retain use of their native language in the home, but too often, social pressures and mistaken beliefs often limit children benefiting from the bilingual brain booster.

One problem is parents' concern that exposure to one language is less confusing for children. When I taught fifth grade in a school where most of the students' primary language was Spanish, I recall recently immigrated parents of my students telling me that although they were just learning English, they tried to only speak English at home with their children. They felt that would help their children learn English more successfully and believed that exposure to two languages would be confusing and make the transition to their new schools more difficult.

Just like our muscles become stronger with physical workouts, the developing brains of children in bilingual environments appear to build strength, speed, and efficiency in their executive function networks.

Another issue limiting the bilingual experiences was children's desire to fit in. As my students' English fluency improved, they would sometimes be asked by their parents to translate from English to Spanish during school conferences or meetings. When they did so, such as during "Back to School

Night," many were clearly embarrassed that their parents didn't speak English and even tried to avoid having classmates hear them speak Spanish to their parents. When I would ask them about their reluctance, some would tell me that it made their parents seem "ignorant" when they did not speak English. My urging of parents to sustain the bilingual experience by speaking Spanish with their children in the home was thus resisted as children began to develop this bias against their native language.

The mistaken parental beliefs about confusing the brain with two languages and the response to their children's negative responses to their native language cause these children to miss out on a unique and powerful opportunity to strengthen their highest cognitive brain potentials. One intervention educators and others in the community can do to avoid loss of the bilingual boost is to explain to new immigrants about the research and the strong impact they can have on their children's academic success by retaining their native language in the home.

A Mistaken Assumption About the Brain

The other intervention is to lay to rest the mistaken assumption that the brain has limitations that are overwhelmed with dual language exposure. The more we learn about neuroplasticity, the more it appears the reverse is true. Experiences with new domains of challenge in general seem to strengthen the brain's executive functions and cognition. This is evident on neuroimaging as well as in performance on the cognitive testing, reading comprehension, and success learning subsequent new languages. New challenges that include the use of judgment, analysis, deduction, translation, prioritizing, attention focusing, inhibitory control, delayed gratification, and pursuit of long-term goals are associated with increasing the number, strength, and efficiency of the executive function networks.

Just like our muscles become stronger with physical workouts, the developing brains of children in bilingual environments appear to build strength, speed, and efficiency in their executive function networks. This is the "neurons that fire together, wire together" phenomenon that in response to the electrical activations of messages traveling through them when used, executive function networks develop stronger connections—dendrites, synapses, and myelinated axons.

For now, it appears that when families have another language that can be spoken in the home where children are being raised it could be an opportunity to both enrich their language skills and also provide a cognitive boost for their highest brain networks of executive functions.

The implications of the bilingual research raise considerations of what other early exposures before and during school years can be designed to promote these executive function activations in all children. What are the implications regarding introducing second languages to young children from monolingual homes? Perhaps grandparents, nannies, friendships with families who speak another language could spend time with the children, or parents could participate in parent-child language classes suitable for youngsters such as learning and singing songs with movements in another language.

14

Let's Stop Pretending That French Is an Important Language

John McWhorter

John McWhorter is associate professor of English and comparative literature at Columbia University and author of Our Magnificent Bastard Tongue: The Untold History of English.

Although bilingual education is invaluable, learning French as a second language does not make sense for most Americans. Children would be better served by becoming bilingual in Spanish, Chinese, or another language that would be more useful than French.

A somewhat surprising piece in *The New York Times* this week reported that the French dual-language program in New York's public school system "is booming," the third-largest such program in the city, after Spanish and Chinese. That commitment is a beautiful thing—for children of Francophone immigrants. But for we natives, the idea that kids need to pick up French is now antique.

Make no mistake: For immigrant kids from anywhere, bilingual education is invaluable. But the idea that American-born children need to learn French has become more reflex than action, like classical music played at the wedding of people who live to modern pop. French in educated America

John McWhorter, "Let's Stop Pretending That French Is an Important Language," *New Republic*, February 2, 2014. Copyright © 2014 New Republic. All rights reserved. Reproduced with permission.

is now a class marker, originating from that distant day when French was Europe's international language.

Fewer Europeans spoke English then, which made French actually useful—at least for Americans who could afford international travel. Those same Americans were also still suffering from an inferiority complex to Europe's "sophistication."

Enter the idea that a language that began as a mere peasant dialect of Latin is a language of precision, savoir-faire, and romance: Molière, Voltaire, Pepe Le Pew. Naturally, then, our little ones must even now know some French to qualify as what used to be called "people of quality."

It's swell that knowing French allows you to ignore subtitles in the occasional art house film, but unclear why this would be considered a priority of childrearing.

But the era of Henry James is long past. When I was a teenaged language nerd in the seventies and eighties, it was the tail end of a time when kids of my bent knew French first and foremost, and then likely dabbled in other Romance languages, plus some German and maybe a dash of Russian. Grand old pop-linguist authors like Mario Pei could write about what they termed the "languages of the world" in books where European languages took up a good half of the space.

After all, between the twenties and the Immigration Act of 1965, immigration to America was lower than it had ever been. Betty Draper and Lucy Ricardo likely never knew a Chinese person in any real way; to them, immigrants were Italians running restaurants. But as *Fiddler on the Roof*'s Tevye had it, "It's a new world, Golde." Somewhere in the nineties, I noticed when teaching linguistics classes that Spanish had overtaken French, and that students were more likely to have studied Japanese, Chinese or Arabic than German or Russian. These are children of the post-Immigration Act era, either by birth or just experience.

What, then, will be a new marker of linguistic classiness? One could be to seek languages for actual use rather than as a fashion statement—i.e. to be more like Europeans, where English has become the international language. One learns French to communicate with . . . who, exactly? Some will yearn to read Sartre and Molière; more power to them. But what about languages like Spanish and Chinese, which are useful to learn because we encounter them in everyday life? I have seen medical professionals just miss getting plum jobs in New York because a competitor happened to speak Spanish, and Chinese will be increasingly important in the business world. Arabic skills, meanwhile, are achingly needed on the geopolitical scene. It's swell that knowing French allows you to ignore subtitles in the occasional art house film, but unclear why this would be considered a priority of childrearing.

And especially with Chinese, beginning to learn the language at 18, in a freshman course, is too late. Someone with a few years of Spanish can often communicate on at least the basic level of Chris Farley's Matt Foley on SNL, but that's much less likely with Chinese. You have to speak each syllable on one of four tones—*bi* can mean *compare, nose, than* or *force* depending on the tone. That's easiest for tots with maximally plastic brains and minimal self-consciousness; later, for many, it is simply impossible. Plus, you have to master a few thousand symbols, most of which resemble nothing in particular except one another, in order to even be able to read a newspaper headline or a children's book. Many adults gamely hoping to learn a little Chinese are defeated by the demands of the characters alone. Kids have more time and less else to focus on, and can learn the symbols more as Chinese kids do.

What, then, is the benefit of kids internalizing *Comment allez-vous?* rather than *¿Como estas?, Nǐ hǎo?*, or even Hindi's *Ap kaise hai?* All I know is that if my two-year-old turns out to be the language nerd I was, I will counsel her to think of French as a distinctly low priority. I'm trying to learn some

Chinese lately. As I laboriously stuff the characters into my head with flash cards and watch natives sweetly wincing as I mangle the tones, I only wish that even as far back as the Watergate era they had been teaching me Chinese instead of the likes of *pomme de terre* and *je m'appelle. Hélas.*

Organizations to Contact

The editors have compiled the following list of organizations concerned with the issues debated in this book. The descriptions are derived from materials provided by the organizations. All have publications or information available for interested readers. The list was compiled on the date of publication of the present volume; the information provided here may change. Be aware that many organizations take several weeks or longer to respond to inquiries, so allow as much time as possible.

California Association for Bilingual Education (CABE)
16033 E San Bernardino Rd., Covina, CA   91722
(626) 814-4441 • fax: (626) 814-4640
e-mail: info@bilingualeducation.org
website: www.bilingualeducation.org

The California Association for Bilingual Education (CABE) is a nonprofit organization that promotes bilingual education and quality educational experiences for all students in California. CABE implements priorities, initiatives, and services targeted to teachers, administrators, parents, and others designed to dramatically increase California's capacity to create culturally diverse and competent learning environments. CABE publishes *The Multilingual Educator.*

Center for Equal Opportunity (CEO)
7700 Leesburg Pike, Suite 231, Falls Church, VA   22043
(703) 442-0066 • fax: (703) 442-0449
website: www.ceousa.org

The Center for Equal Opportunity (CEO) is the nation's only conservative think tank devoted to issues of race and ethnicity. CEO opposes admission, hiring, and contracting policies that discriminate, sort, or prefer on the basis of race or ethnicity; and it opposes bilingual education. CEO publishes a variety of articles, many of which are available online.

English First Foundation

8001 Forbes Place, Suite 102, Springfield, VA   22151
(703) 321-8818 • fax: (703) 321-7636
website: www.englishfirstfoundation.org

The English First Foundation aims to educate the public about the importance of preserving English as the common language of the United States. The English First Foundation aggressively seeks out opportunities to weigh in during the approval process for various federal regulations. The English First Foundation distributes pro-English books free of charge to school libraries.

Intercultural Development Research Association (IDRA)

5815 Callaghan Rd., Suite 101, San Antonio, TX   78228
(210) 444-1710 • fax: (210) 444-1714
e-mail: feedback@idra.org
website: www.idra.org

The Intercultural Development Research Association (IDRA) is an independent, nonprofit organization that is dedicated to assuring educational opportunity for every child. IDRA is a vocal advocate for the right of every student to equality of educational opportunity. IDRA publishes a monthly newsletter and has a variety of publications available at its website.

National Association for Bilingual Education (NABE)

11006 Veirs Mill Rd., #L-1, Wheaton, MD   20902
(240) 450-3700 • fax: (240) 450-3799
e-mail: nabe@nabe.org
website: www.nabe.org

The National Association for Bilingual Education (NABE) is a nonprofit membership organization that works to ensure that language-minority students have equal opportunities to learn English and succeed academically. NABE aims to improve instructional practices for linguistically and culturally diverse children. NABE publishes the bimonthly periodical *Perspectives.*

ProEnglish

1601 N Kent St., Suite 1100, Arlington, VA   22209
(703) 816-8821 • fax: (571) 527-2813
e-mail: email@proenglish.org
website: www.proenglish.org

ProEnglish is an advocate of official English. ProEnglish works through the courts and in the court of public opinion to defend English's historic role as America's common, unifying language, and to persuade lawmakers to adopt English as the official language at all levels of government. ProEnglish opposes bilingual education and has a variety of articles at its website explaining its position on English in the United States.

U.S. English Foundation, Inc.

2000 L St. NW, Suite 702, Washington, DC   20036
(202) 833-0100 • fax: (202) 833-0108
e-mail: info@usenglish.org
website: www.usefoundation.org

The U.S. English Foundation contends that learning English quickly and learning it with English-speaking peers is the best way for English learners to get ahead economically, academically, and socially. The organization aims to improve the teaching of English to immigrants, conduct research on language issues and policies, and raise public awareness about the importance of a common language. The foundation has a variety of publications available at its website, including "E Pluribus Unum: Out of Many, One . . . Why English as a Common Language Is Critical to America's Unity."

Bibliography

Books

Sara M. Beaudrie and Marta Fairclough, eds. *Spanish as a Heritage Language in the United States: The State of the Field.* Washington, DC: Georgetown University Press, 2012.

Karen Beeman and Cheryl Urow *Teaching for Biliteracy: Strengthening Bridges Between Languages.* Philadelphia: Caslon Publishing, 2013.

Rebecca M. Callahan and Patricia C. Gándara *Bilingual Advantage: Language, Literacy, and the US Labor Market.* Buffalo, NY: Multilingual Matters, 2014.

Patricia Gándara and Megan Hopkins *English Learners and Restrictive Language Policies.* New York: Teachers College Press, 2010.

Paul C. Gorski and Kristien Zenkov *The Big Lies of School Reform: Finding Better Solutions for the Future of Public Education.* New York: Routledge, 2014.

Carollee Howes, Jason T. Downer, and Robert C. Pianta, eds. *Dual Language Learners in the Early Childhood Classroom.* Baltimore, MD: Paul H. Brookes, 2011.

Bryant Jensen and Adam Sawyer, eds. *Regarding Education: Mexican-American Schooling, Immigration, and the Bi-National Improvement.* New York: Teachers College Press, 2013.

David L. Kirp — *Improbable Scholars: The Rebirth of a Great American School System and a Strategy for America's Schools.* New York: Oxford University Press, 2013.

Marguerite Lukes — *Latino Immigrant Youth and Interrupted Schooling: Dropouts, Dreamers and Alternative Pathways to College.* Buffalo, NY: Multilingual Matters, 2015.

Grace P. McField, ed. — *The Miseducation of English Learners: A Tale of Three States and Lessons to Be Learned.* Charlotte, NC: Information Age Publishing, 2014.

John E. Petrovic — *International Perspectives on Bilingual Education.* Charlotte, NC: Information Age Publishing, 2010.

Paul J. Ramsey — *The Bilingual School in the United States.* Charlotte, NC: Information Age Publishing, 2012.

Patricia Ruggiano Schmidt and Althier M. Lazar, eds. — *Practicing What We Teach: How Culturally Responsive Literacy Classrooms Make a Difference.* New York: Teachers College Press, 2011.

John W. Schwieter, ed. — *Innovative Research and Practices in Second Language Acquisition and Bilingualism.* Philadelphia: John Benjamins Publishing Company, 2013.

Touorizou Hervé Somé and Pierre W. Orelus, eds.
Immigration and Schooling: Redefining the 21st Century America. Charlotte, NC: Information Age Publishing, 2015.

Androula Yiakoumetti
Harnessing Linguistic Variation to Improve Education. New York: Peter Lang, 2012.

Periodicals and Internet Sources

Sarah Carr
"Bilingual Education: The Reinvention of Bilingual Education in America's Schools," *Slate,* January 5, 2015. www.slate.com.

Linda Chavez
"Bilingual Education Idiocy in California," *New York Post,* June 6, 2014.

Claudia Dreifus
"The Bilingual Advantage," *New York Times,* May 30, 2011.

Olga Escamilla
"Best of Both Worlds," *Skipping Stones,* May–August 2012.

Libia S. Gil
"Real Equality in Education Remains Elusive," *National Journal,* June 5, 2014.

Mike Gonzalez
"The Big Lie We Tell 'English Learners,'" *New York Post,* October 8, 2014.

François Grosjean
"What Are the Effects of Bilingualism?," *Psychology Today,* June 16, 2011. www.psychologytoday.com.

Jeffrey M. Jones   "Most in US Say It's Essential that
                          Immigrants Learn English," Gallup,
                          August 9, 2013. www.gallup.com.

Jeffrey Kluger   "How the Brain Benefits from Being
                          Bilingual," *Time*, July 18, 2013.

Stacey J. Lee   "New Talk About ELL Students," *Phi
                          Delta Kappan*, May 2012.

Clifford J. Levy   "Strangers in a Strange School," *New
                          York Times Magazine*, September 18,
                          2011.

Caroline Linse   "Linguistic Capital Pays Dividends,"
                          Phi Delta Kappan, March 2013.

Los Angeles Times   "Is Bilingual Education Worth
                          Bringing Back?" June 4, 2014.

Matthew Lynch   "Why Bilingual Education Should Be
                          Mandatory," *Education Week*,
                          November 10, 2014.
                          http://blogs.edweek.org.

Rubén Martinez   "The Mother Tongues: Learning
                          Spanish and English Unites
                          Children," *Los Angeles Times*, April
                          24, 2011.

Lillian Mongeau   "Bilingual Education Could Make a
                          Comeback," *EdSource*, July 29, 2014.
                          www.edsource.org.

Rosalie P. Porter   "Bill to End Ban on Bilingual
                          Education Hurts Immigrant Kids,"
                          San Francisco Chronicle, September
                          17, 2014.

Ryan J. Smith   "California's Public Schools Are
                     Failing English Learners," *Sacramento
                     Bee*, January 22, 2015.

Mary A. Stewart   "Opinion: Why Is Bilingual
                     Education Better?," Fox News Latino,
                     June 25, 2014.
                     http://latino.foxnews.com.

Valerie Strauss   "Why Is Bilingual Education 'Good'
                     for Rich Kids but 'Bad' for Poor,
                     Immigrant Students?," *Washington
                     Post*, October 24, 2014.

Teresa Watanabe   "Dual-Language Immersion
                     Programs Growing in Popularity," *Los
                     Angeles Times*, May 8, 2011.

Conor P. Williams   "Chaos for Dual Language Learners,"
                     New America Foundation, September
                     2014. www.newamerica.org.

Index

CPSIA information can be obtained
at www.ICGtesting.com
Printed in the USA
FFOW05n0740120116